Rock ★ Star
Customer Service
Program

6 Secrets To Rock Star Customer Service

I0394056

Written By:
Coach David Brownlee

 **by**
PURE **Customer Service**
The world's best customer service training. **Guaranteed.**

©2013 Pure Customer Service

ROCK STAR
CUSTOMER SERVICE

6 SECRETS TO ROCK STAR CUSTOMER SERVICE

By

David Brownlee

TABLE OF CONTENTS

PREFACE

I am David Brownlee, founder of **Pure Customer Service** and creator of **The Rock Star Customer Service Training Program**. Before we start, I just want to say thank you for choosing the **Rock Star Customer Service Training** to improve your customer service skills and knowledge. Whether it's to increase your customer database, improve your online reviews, increase your revenues and grow your business, or even to get that promotion or pay raise in your customer service job.

Whatever your reason, I commend you for taking the time to read this book, to better your skills, and to continue learning. I hope that you get great value out of this writing.

Customer service is my passion. I'm lucky to be training on this subject every day. I absolutely love it! Throughout my career, I've worked in several businesses, from large Fortune 500 companies to restaurants and small businesses. The one thing that I found in any successful business, big or small, is that customer service is the key to a company's success. Specifically, Rock Star Customer Service is the key to a company's success.

What do I mean by that? Imagine for a moment that you are going about your daily business as usual when you get a phone call. Mick Jagger (or Paul McCartney- Stones vs. Beatles) is interested in your company. They need your product or service. Or better yet, they actually come into your place of business and need your help that you can provide them. After you "come to" from fainting and wipe the drool off your mouth (fellas, this exercise works with Beyoncé or fill in the blank), what would you say to them? How would you treat them? What length would you go to in order to make sure they are well taken care of? How would you entice them to tell their famous friends about you and your company? What would you offer them to come back? I'm guessing the service you strive to provide them would be pretty stellar.

The idea of doing business with rock stars can be an exciting thought. To me, an even more exciting thought is treating your customers that come into your business everyday like rock stars. They will tell all of their friends (famous or not) how great you and your business are. They will come back to your business over and over again.

They will write great things about you online for the world to see resulting in raving fan clients that are excited to do business with you.

You may be thinking, "But David, I run a small business and I don't have the tools, time or money to implement a customer service program like the big companies to create raving fan customers." Here's the good news. You don't have to. Creating raving fan clients is easier than ever to do. It's not expensive either. In this book, you'll learn how to gain client referrals, get more positive online reviews, increase your sales and grow your business.

Without customers, your business can't exist, right? At least, not for very long.

Over the years, I've started and sold numerous businesses in different industries, and have always done my best to implement the strategies I've learned and the tools I've discovered. These are the same concepts that you will be learning throughout this course. I've had the pleasure of training thousands of people in customer service, and I'm excited to continue doing so with you.

This training will help you increase your revenues, build a loyal customer base, increase customer referrals, and get more positive online reviews. And if you're a customer service representative, they will definitely help you to be better, more confident, and more successful in your job, and hopefully enhance your career.

Thanks for reading, and enjoy.

To book your next live training event with Coach David Brownlee, call or visit our website today!

(800) 299-3449

PureCustomerService.com

DavidBrownlee.com

CHAPTER 1

ROCK STAR CUSTOMER SERVICE OVERVIEW

I live in a little beach community in San Diego right now, and the other day, I wanted to have some Chinese food. I was sitting on the couch, feeling a little bit lazy, I don't really want to get up and go anywhere, so I thought to myself that I should see if I can get some Chinese delivery to the house. You'd figure in a beach town, there'd be all types of Chinese delivery, right? But I was having trouble finding one that can deliver to the house. I decided to go onto Yelp.com, I found one Chinese restaurant that delivers to my area. I call them up, all excited, and said, "I'd like some chicken chow mean, and I'd like that delivered." He said, "Well, you know what, there's a $15 minimum for delivery." I told him that was okay. It makes sense to have a minimum order amount in the food delivery industry. They have to pay their delivery guy; they have the cost of gas, etc. So I told him to give me some egg rolls with that, and some soup.

My total came to $14.98. I said, "$14.98? That's perfect, we hit it right on the nose." And he said, well, there's $15 minimum order. And I said again, "That's great, we've got it, we're at $14.98, we hit it, and how did we get so close?" He said, well, there's a $15 minimum order. And I thought he was kidding at first because I just couldn't believe it. I asked him what he wanted me to do, thinking he would bust out in laughter and say, "Gotcha!" But that's not what happened. He said, "Well, you have to order something else or we won't deliver." I told him we were literally talking about two cents. "Two cents, can you deliver my food to me?" His answer was no. Needless to say I was dumbfounded AND pissed.

And if you think about this, here's a guy who is the only Chinese food delivery in this area. He can OWN the Chinese delivery market. Even with marginal customer service, he would dominate the market. But we got hung up on two cents. And you know what happened at the end of that? I got in my car and drove down the street to a different Chinese restaurant. At least this exchange got me off the couch to go and do it. I couldn't believe it. Two cents, are you kidding me? Especially nowadays, with sites like Yelp, Trip Advisor, Google Reviews and other online review sites, you have to start looking at the big picture. What's this customer going to do after interacting with my company? How much is that customer worth to my business long term? These are some things we're going to take a look at today. The owner of that Chinese restaurant should have known that I would have been a loyal customer, told my friends and would have become a raving fan...if the food was good. I love Chinese.

Getting started, what will you learn today? Well, we're going to take a look at some myths that surround customer service, because there are some customer service myths that are preventing businesses from being their best. Next, we're going to answer the question, Why is a customer so important? Then, we'll explore the importance of positive communication with customers. Finally, we're going to learn the meaning of the acronym PURE CS (Pure Customer Service).

CHAPTER 2

Customer Service Myths

LET'S take a look at the THREE MYTHS surrounding customer service. The FIRST MYTH is, "It's impossible to give great customer service all the time." A lot of business owners and customer service representatives have adopted this way of thinking. You just can't give a great customer service all the time. You may get upset customers over some things that aren't your fault that happen, and they're really heated up. But don't give up and resolve yourself to believe that there is no way to handle this effectively. I'm going to show you that you can do it. You can give great customer service all the time, especially with the clients that are having problems with your customer service or your product, and that's going to be really great to share with you. In fact, the more irate your customer, the bigger the opportunity to turn that customer into a loyal, raving fan for life.

The SECOND MYTH is that customers are too demanding. This is a very common feeling among business owners, executives and customer service professionals.

Customers are too demanding. I can already see you nodding your head in agreement. It's a justifiable feeling since we as a culture want everything now. We want it better than it was before. We want everything faster than we got it before. When you start thinking about how customer service has evolved from where it was 20 years ago to where it is now, a lot has changed. Thanks to technology, the sheer speed at which we can get products and services is astounding. I'll give you an example. Last year, I went to a wedding in Paris. I was walking around the shopping district with a buddy of mine and I noticed he had this really cool backpack. I told him it was a cool looking backpack and that I was in the market for one myself. He told me about how great it is, and we moved on. Once we were back in the states, I had forgotten about our backpack conversation. A few days later, I got an email from my friend with a link to the backpack online. It was 50% off, so I decided to buy it and ordered it online to be delivered at my house.

This was around five o'clock. I logged in, put my credit card information, and figured I'd see it in a few days. The next morning at 9am, there's like a knock on my door. I wondered who could be coming over at 9am in the morning knocking at my door. It was the delivery guy with that backpack that I ordered 16 hours earlier. I was astonished. THAT was customer service! Super easy and fast. Are customers more demanding? Maybe, but as professionals, we have to take a look at what customer's expectations are and how can we accommodate them; or better yet, exceed them. If we are prepared on the front in and take the needed time to anticipate their needs and build systems around those needs, we will serve our customers at the highest level without feeling like they're too demanding.

The THIRD MYTH is, "In my industry, customer service is not that important to my business or my bottom line." Studies show that it takes four to six times more money to attract a new customer than to keep an old customer, and that affects the bottom line dramatically. Not only that, once you add in your company's profit margins, how much revenue do you actually need to generate to hit that number? For example, if you spend $1,000.00 a month on advertising and you operate on a 50% margin, then you actually have to earn $2,000.00 in revenue to cover that cost. Most companies operate on much less depending on the industry. When you have a customer that really loves your service and they keep coming back for more, and they tell their friends to come. Now you've just picked up FREE customers. Another paying customer that walks through your door ready for a great experience with your company, if those customers love your service that effect continues to compound and grow your business exponentially. And that's huge for any business.

To book your next live training event with Coach David Brownlee, call or visit our website today!

(800) 299-3449

PureCustomerService.com

DavidBrownlee.com

CHAPTER 3

Why Is Customer Service So Important?

WHY is customer service so important? Well, it's the best way to distinguish your business. We're going to talk about how you can distinguish your business through your service. Review websites are everywhere, and more popular than ever. This is a compelling reason why your customer service needs to be on par. Customers allow a business to exist. It's a pretty simple concept; no customers, no business. It's really that simple. Your customers are the most important part of that business. Next, customers are your livelihood, and we're going to talk about how customers help you do your everyday things through giving you a job, a paycheck, and why they're so important.

Customer service is the best way to distinguish your business from your competition. A lot of products and services nowadays, in different categories, are similar. They have similar qualities, similar pricing, etc. What is going to make people come to your business over the other businesses similar to yours, it's the customer service. Ask yourself, "How do you make your customers feel? Do they feel welcomed? Are they getting what they came for? Do they feel like they're getting value out of what you're offering them?" You need to make sure you have the right answers to those questions. We're going to look at the strategies that make sure you get positive answers to these questions.

David Brownlee

Review websites are everywhere and more popular than ever. For example, I was in Playa del Carmen, and we were there for yet another wedding. I've got some buddies getting married in some great spots! I got some great vacation time. So we're in Playa del Carmen and we were walking down the street, and we were trying to figure out where to have a dinner. There are literally hundreds of restaurants on both sides of the street. We had to decide where to go.

We pulled out our smart phones and looked at Trip Advisor. We found some restaurants with some great reviews, and some with not so great reviews. We ended up picking one with a great review; we went there and had a great meal. We loved it. Now, we did see another place from the street that looked great. Before we went in to get a table, we looked it up on Trip Advisor; it had something like two stars. We decided that we are not going anywhere near there. The reviews said the food and the service was terrible. That was all it took to take our business elsewhere. Are people making decisions to skip your business based on your online reviews?

That's why these review sites are really becoming important. When your prospective customer reads positive reviews on your business, they are more likely to give you a shot vs. companies that have poor reviews. If you deliver amazing service and create a raving fan out of that customer, studies show that they will tell three people how great you and your business are.

If you deliver amazing service to those three, then those three people may tell three more people if they have a great experience, and so on. That is the compounding effect of referrals and the best way to grow your business. On the flip side, when people have bad service, studies show that

14

they will tell nine people how crappy your business is. Nowadays with Yelp, one person puts up a review on your business, and bam! Now, thousands of people can now see that you have a bad review on Yelp. Thousands, maybe millions, depending on what company it is, and what people are searching for. That's why this concept is so important to understand.

Positive reviews can obviously boost the number of customers that are going to contact you. They may come through your door, call you, or somehow try your service. And these review sites are very SEO-friendly, so if somebody is looking for your type of business in Yelp or even in Google, your Yelp reviews may come up in the search. If you've gotten nice four or five shiny stars up there, it's going to look good and your prospects are more likely to do business with you.

Your customers allow your business to exist. What do I mean by that? Business is the activity of making, buying, or selling goods, providing services, etc., in exchange for money. It's easy to understand. No customers, no business. Customers are everything to your business, so you want them to feel special. Sincerely tell them thank you every time you come in contact with them. Your customers are the reason you make a profit (or not). Your customers are your livelihood. They provide you with employment and give you the opportunity to have a job. Pay raises, advances-your customers. The more customers that pass through your business the more your business is going to thrive. The more your business thrives the more possibilities in your job for pay raises and advancement.

Customers help you pay your bills. When you're writing that rent check, or you're writing that car payment, think about those customers that give you the job that gives you the business, so you can pay your bills and contribute to your livelihood.

What are you doing to improve your customer service? No matter how good your customer service is now, it can always be better. There are three F's to enhance your customer experience (some of the F's you're thinking about are not in there).

The first F stand for FASTER. How can we make our service faster? How many of you have ever heard from customers, "Hey, this is taking too long." Ask yourself, "Can our service be faster?" The second F is FRIENDLIER. You need to master the ways you can make your service friendlier. You'll get some great strategies in this book. The third F is for FANTASTIC. How can you make your service more fantastic? How can we really wow them? When your customers come through the door, they say, "Wow, I'm always coming back and I'm going to tell everybody to come here.

This is the greatest place on earth! This place is even better than Disneyland!" Okay, that's a bit dramatic but you get the point. You need to figure out how to deliver faster, friendlier and more fantastic service.

CHAPTER 4

The Importance of Positive Communication

NEXT, we're going to talk about communication. Communication takes place between co-workers, staff, management, owners, and customers. Positive communication moves individuals towards their goals or happiness. If someone comes to you with a need and you help provide him or her with a solution, then you have contributed to him or her positively through communication. When your customers come to you with a problem or a need, and you can come up with a solution for those customers in a friendly manner, you're going to be winning.

How can you say YES to your customers more often than saying no? I have a 14-month-old son and he's now learning how to walk. His walking around is kind of' funny, and getting into all sorts of things that he's not supposed to. He's starting to open cabinets, climb everything on sight and throw his prized possessions into the toilet.
He has a ball! Do you know what I'm talking about? If you have ever had or known little ones running around, at some point they WILL start getting into everything. There soon comes the day that you have to start telling them "No!" to keep them safe. And then it begins. A lifetime of hearing "No!"

The other day I was in the kitchen getting my son's Sippy cup for him while he was in the dining room waiting for me. Not 10 seconds later, I came back to find him sitting on the dining room table, laughing hysterically as he dumped water from a glass onto my laptop while precariously balanced on the edge of the table. Can you say, CPS? A million things went through my head at that moment. First, I wanted to grab him to keep him from falling off the table, and then I thought of all of my work on my laptop, etc. It was absolute chaos. I had to start yelling "No, no, no!" That's when it starts. It starts when we're little and continues on as we grow up. As you get older, you hear it more and more, "No!" From our teachers, bosses, our spouses and yes, companies we do business with. Somebody please just tell us "YES!"

When your customers make requests of you, "Can I get extra fries with that," or "Can I get more cheese on that," or "Can I do xyz?" Think of ways you can say YES. Sometimes you can't say yes (see above example with baby on the table), but try to think of creative ways that you can say "NO." It's always kind of fun to think of alternatives. Challenge your team and staff to really think of creative ways to say "No" that preserve positive communication between you and your customers. For example, instead of saying "No", you could say, "Well, I wish I could, but let me tell you what I CAN do." Instead of saying "No", try to figure out an alternative that's in the positive, and make it a positive communication. Does that makes sense? What are some ways you can say "NO" to YOUR customers and keep the interaction positive?

What is this positive communication anyway? There are two types of communication.

There's verbal, and there's non-verbal. Verbal communication includes the words that you say. The words you say to your customers are very powerful. They're going to be asking themselves, "What exactly are you telling me? "Are you telling me you're going to help me?" "Do you want to help me?" "Are you a friendly person that cares about me?" How your clients answer these questions in their heads is going to make a difference on whether or not they do business with you and enjoy their experience. How you say it can be even more important than what you say in some instances.

The tone in which you say something will impact how your customer perceives the interaction. When you first welcome your customers, make sure you and you staff are smiling. Show an attitude of happiness and warmth. Welcome your customers in person or on the phone with a smile, great attitude and a welcoming tone.

The second type of communication is non-verbal communication. Your facial expressions and body language are examples of non-verbal communication. Here is another baby example; obviously I have babies on my mind at this stage of my life). Whenever you look at a baby, you see the baby staring back at you and studying you. What the baby is doing is reading your face because we're all born with this instinct and ability to read people's faces. The baby will stare at you to determine if you are happy, sad, angry or threatening in some way. They're looking for anything to tell them how to react to you in a given situation. Even as adults, we are constantly doing the same thing subconsciously. When someone walks into your establishment make sure that you're smiling so you can send a positive communication to them immediately.

Be aware of what your face look like. You could be frowning even if you are not explicitly angry. People pick up on non-verbal communication instantly.

Be aware of your body language during customer interactions. Are your arms crossed? Are you holding your cell phone in your hand? Are you disinterested in your client and busy texting? That last one is my pet peeve. Have you ever walked in somewhere and somebody's texting and without looking up they say, "Oh, hey. Can I help you?" There should be a universal rule that the customer has the right to take the offender's phone and toss it out the nearest window. Texting in the workplace and checking Facebook is a huge trend right now that needs to stop. Next, what is your appearance like when you interact with clients? How do you look? Do you have a uniform? Are you wearing dirty and disheveled clothing? How's your hygiene? Are your nails clean? Do you smell funny? Customers will absolutely pick up on those pretty quick.

The single most important part of communication is building rapport. What do I mean by that and what is rapport? Rapport is something you have in common with someone else. If two people are similar in some way or perceive that they are similar to someone in some way, rapport is built. Rapport is the foundation for any positive relationship between individuals. How does that apply to customer service in my business? Let's say a customer of yours is wearing a sweatshirt from a university. I may say, "Oh wow, my sister went to the same university, that's a great school." Then, bam! Rapport is built and now you have the foundation of a positive relationship that can be built upon during your interaction. Be sincere and have fun with it.

Depending on your business and how much time you have to actually spend with the customer, you can determine how much rapport building time you'll have with them. Other things you can talk about that build rapport are children, sports, current events, etc. Just about anything can be used to build rapport as long as there is a perceived commonality. Try to talk about general topics or an observance. General topics are something like the weather or clothing. "Hey, it's really hot out there today, especially for this time of the year, right?" Or, "It's hot out there, you staying cool?" Two subjects to avoid at all costs are politics and religion, if you can. Those conversations can go downhill real quickly, so you just want to keep it light.

Always acknowledge the customer. How many of you have experienced a line, where people are waiting and they're getting agitated because they have been waiting for a long time and see no end in sight. Have you seen that? A lot of times, somebody comes into an establishment and is made to wait in line. Simply have you or one of your staff acknowledged them so that they know they are important and you actually care that they are waiting for your product or service. You can say, "Hi, how are you? I'll be with you just in a second." If they won't hear you, give a head nod in acknowledgement, smile and hold up a finger (mind which finger). Smile and mouth to them that you'll be with them shortly. This tells the client "Hey, you're important, and someone will get to you as soon as possible. This is extremely important. How can you implement this concept in your business?

TO BOOK YOUR NEXT LIVE TRAINING EVENT WITH DAVID BROWNLEE, CALL OR VISIT OUR WEBSITE TODAY!

(800) 299-3449

PureCustomerService.com

DavidBrownlee.com

CHAPTER 5

<u>Step 1:</u>   PURE CS - P Is For Psychology

WHAT does the acronym PURE CS stand for? I love acronyms, so I came up with an acronym for Pure Customer Service. The P is for Psychology. We need to ask ourselves, "What is the psychology of our customers?" "What is the psychology of our company?" "What is our personal psychology about?" **Psychology** is the mental or behavioral characteristics of an individual or group. So how does psychology play a key role in customer service? We're going to look at it from the perspective of three different groups in the company, the customer, and the customer service professionals themselves.

When you take a look at your company, what are the values of your company? You need to be crystal clear on this and how it translates to your customers, employees, and vendors. What is your company's mission statement and how does it relate to your customer service policies and procedures? What is it that we internalize about your company and attach to your brand? The Ritz-Carlton's whole business is built around the customer experience. When we think of the Ritz-Carlton we think of amazing customer service. The customer is the most important part of that company. Nordstrom, another great customer-centric company, is based around serving the customer to the highest level. Enterprise Rent-a-Car is one of the biggest privately held companies in the world. Their aim is to take such great care of their customers that they will come back again, and again. These companies know what they are doing and are the best in the world at making the customer feel appreciated, important and cared for.

Your company's values come through to your customers, staff and vendors via the owners and the management. These values dictate how you treat your customers and the value that your company puts on the customer. Zappos is another company that understands the importance of their customers and treat their customers like rock stars. What are the mantras and mission statements of your company's culture? Do you have one? Do you know what it is? This will have the single biggest effect on your customer service professionals and support staff. Through this trickle down culture, your customers are at the end of this chain and you need to be sure they are getting the right message and experience from your company as intended. If you do not have a mission statement and values for your company, do not go another day without putting an in-depth, clear mission statement and value statement together and make sure everyone knows what it is. That is the foundation to dramatically change your business for the better.

Your customers want THREE things from your company when it comes to customer service. The first thing your clients want is TO BE HEARD.

When your clients come to you to buy your company's product or service, they want to know you will deliver what they wanted and expected. Next, your customers want TO BE UNDERSTOOD. Do you really understand what I'm trying to get from your company? How do you make absolute sure that you understand? You ask them intelligent questions. For example, if you're making a smoothie for a customer and this is their first time to your store. If they are not sure what to get, ask them questions to fully understand what they want. You might ask, "Do you like berries?" Do you want something sweet? Do you like strawberries? Are you allergic to any berries? You ask them questions to get the information so that you are exactly sure what they're looking for and wanted.

Next, they want TO BE CARED FOR. They want to know that they're important and their patronage is valued. Even if a customer shows up in a sour mood because they've had a bad day, you can brighten their day in an instant through a smile, kind words and rapport building. Let them know and feel comfortable in the fact that you are going to take care of them now despite what may have happened earlier in their day before they entered your establishment.

What is your psychology when it comes to customers? Customer service is all about attitude. What's your attitude towards your customers? We talked about how important they are, so how do you show them? They need to know that you appreciate them and that you will do everything you can to make them feel welcome and provide a solution for them. You start to do this through your attitude. As you smile, you may say something like, "Thank you for coming." Or, "Thank you for choosing our service (your business name her)." You might say, "How can I help you?" Anything you say to the customer is sincere because they can sense when you're not. Remember to have a welcoming tone of voice and a smile.

Excellent, rock star customer service starts with a positive attitude! The most important concept to remember is another acronym, because I love acronyms, SEC. It's called SEC because it's only takes a sec or a second to do. There are three elements to it.

The first element is to SMILE. Whenever you interact with a customer always greet them with a smile. You greet them with a smile because smiles are contagious. If you smiling at somebody they will most likely smile back at you. It's an instinct. When you smile at them, you are letting them know that you have a positive attitude and ready to serve them. When a smiling representative of a company that appears happy and glad to see you, greets you, you'll instinctively smile back. You're ready for your interaction with this company. Even if you've had a crappy day, if the rep does it right, you will smile back. You may realize, oh I'm grumpy and consciously wipe that grin off your face, but your instinct is to smile back. Even if you are grumpy, we expect subconsciously to be greeted by customer service reps, salespeople, and servers in restaurants, with a smile. Service with a smile is key. We expect it. We crave it. It's getting harder and harder to find companies willing to give it to us. For example, I fly a lot.

And with everything that has been going on with the airlines these days, with budget cuts, flight delays, increased security, etc., those folks that work for the airlines from front desk to flight attendants aren't the nicest people to deal with. I understand that they are under paid and there is lack of job security but a simple smile and greeting would make all of the difference in the world. Even if they say the right thing, without a smile it doesn't make you feel exactly warm and fuzzy inside.
This is HUGE.

The second element is to MAKE EYE CONTACT. Make eye contact with your clients during your interactions. Eye contact shows that you are ready to engage them and help them in some way. It shows you care about what they are and are ready to connect and serve them. It also shows that you're listening to them. Make sure you use eye contact in combination with the smile. You don't want to freak anybody out. Smile and make eye contact. It sounds simple because it is. Yet more often than not, companies miss this crucial piece.

Next, make a POSITIVE COMMENT or COMPLIMENT to your customers. For example, if you greet somebody with a piece of jewelry that you like you may say, "That's a pretty necklace." Just make it sincere and be careful! Keep your comments and compliments classy. This is especially important for the fellas. If you have a female customer, keep it classy, not creepy. That's important. You could comment on the weather, light-hearted current events, etc.

TO BOOK YOUR NEXT LIVE TRAINING EVENT WITH DAVID BROWNLEE, CALL OR VISIT OUR WEBSITE TODAY!

(800) 299-3449

PureCustomerService.com

DavidBrownlee.com

CHAPTER 6

Step 2: U Is For Understanding

NEXT, the U in PURE CS is for understanding. There are three skills you need to perfect when it comes to understanding your customers. One is, ASK INTELLIGENT QUESTIONS. That's how you make sure you're providing the right product and the right service for your customer. You need to clearly understand their needs, wants and expectations from you, your company and your product or service. If your client is unclear, ask questions so that you can make intelligent suggestions to your clients. You are the expert, you know your products, and you know your services, so go ahead and suggest the best solution for them. They'll appreciate that you took the time to understand their true desires and offer solutions for them.

Two, is TO LISTEN INTENTLY. This is crucial to do with all of your customers. It is important during routine transactions, but it is especially important when a customer approaches you with a problem they are having. While they are explaining the problem or complaint they are having, listen and connect with the customer. Really take the time to understand what they're saying and why. A lot of times, especially if they're a really heated customer, if you take the time to listen to them, that is all it takes to make them feel better. It sounds too good to be true but it is! All of your customers WANT TO BE HEARD, remember? If you let them vent when they're heated, sometimes that is all it takes to alleviate the problem or complaint. They might even say to you afterwards, "I'm sorry I got so upset with you." You may respond, "I understand, it happens." And just like that, the client feels better and is ready to do business with you again. It's like magic without the hat and the rabbit.

Three, PICK UP ON VERBAL AND NON-VERBAL CUES. There are subtle verbal cues that you need to be able to pick up on in order to make sure your customer is happy. Sometimes customers will make an INDIRECT OBJECTION or side comment about you, your product, your service or your company. They may not want direct confrontation, so they avoid making a big deal about it, but you need to address it. For example, a client might say, "Hmmm, that's pretty expensive." Rather than "gloss over" the comment, address it. Say something along the lines of, "What were you expecting to pay for x?" "The reason X is more expensive than other X's is that we use the highest quality ingredients and it is the highest quality product you can get."

An example of NON-VERBAL CUES are frowning, looking away, shaking their head or sighing. Tactfully address these cues. Ask, "Is this what you were expecting?" "Is everything the way you wanted it?" Try to get out exactly what it is that the customer is upset or disappointed about. You may offer, "Is there something else that might suit you better?" Your power to ensure that the customer has a great experience with your company is while you are in their presence. Never let a customer leave unhappy.

CHAPTER 7

Step 3: R Is For Response/ Responsibility

R is for RESPONSE AND RESPOSIBILITY. How do you RESPOND to your customers when they make a request? Are you friendly? Are you ready to help, and engage them? Make sure that you respond appropriately to your customers' needs and concerns, and take responsibility in that moment for your company's service.
What do these terms mean?

First, let's look at the RESPONSE. The response must be appropriate to the interaction with the customer. For example, if somebody is upset and explaining to you about their problem and you're smiling at them, which is not appropriate for that situation. But David, you said to ALWAYS greet a customer with a smile? Yes, but as soon as you sense they are upset and they start unleashing complaints, show EMPATHY and respond accordingly (more on EMPATHY later). You don't want to smile too long. You might get punched out. If a client is telling you about something that's really bothering them and you have a silly grin plastered on your face, it could be well Bam! Lights out. You get the picture. Make sure your RESPONSE is appropriate to the situation.

Second, let's look at RESPONSIBILITY. At some point you will most likely encounter a client that is NOT upset with you directly but rather with your co-worker, your company, the product or service and it's not your fault directly. In that moment YOU represent the company. You absolutely 100%, in that moment take responsibility for whatever problem or issue that the client is having. I know it does not seem fair, but here's the reality. You do not need to take offense to the challenge, but you do need to take RESPONSIBILITY for the challenge and do everything in your possession to solve it. You might say, "I'm so sorry that this happened. I apologize. Let me get started on this right away to make this right for you." Or, "What can I do to make this better for you?" That's taking responsibility, and your customers will appreciate it if you get them the desired results. Do not waste time, just get on it and find a solution that makes the customer happy.

Next, reassure the customer that you will take care of them. If they do have a problem, depending on your company's policies, they may have to wait for a manager. That's okay if that's part of your procedures, but let them know, "I'll be here every step of the way." For example, if you're in a hotel and your light bulb doesn't work, and you go down to the front desk and you tell them about the problem.
They're most likely not going to go up and change it themselves, but they will call someone from maintenance to do it for you. Rock Star Customer Service entails the customer service representative being there for the client until the problem gets resolved. That may sound like, "If it doesn't get done in the next 10 minutes, please give me a call, and I'll make sure that it gets done right away.

I'm going to be your point of contact, even though I'm not going to be the one changing it, I'm going to make sure that it gets done for you." You are RESPONSIBLE to solve your customers' issue no matter who is at fault.

Next, respond QUICKLY and with PURPOSE. When a client tells you about an issue that they're having, don't push them off and make them wait too long while you try and figure everything out. Your client has better things to do than to watch you think.

Show them that you are attentive and taking action to alleviate the problem. For example, if you work in a smoothie shop and somebody gets a drink that they didn't like, or a smoothie that they don't like, take it from them immediately to get them one they LOVE. Take it and ask, "What was it about this drink that you don't like?" LISTEN, make sure you UNDERSTAND what they want and make them a new one in that moment. Don't make them wait, don't make them wonder, just get to it and deliver exactly what they wanted. This will have a huge impact on how they feel CARED FOR. Are you starting to see how all of these concepts are starting to come together?

Remember to RESPOND positively whenever you can. And we talk about this a lot, positivity, positivity, positivity! There are specific ways to do that. First, SMILE. Second, try to use language that's in the affirmative by saying YES instead of NO. Third, try to find out alternative ways to meet your clients' needs through OPTIONS, which we will discuss in more details in later chapters.

Next, when you take REPONSIBILITY for the situation, whether or not it's your fault, never get defensive or take the customer's dissatisfaction personally. It's not you they are upset with, it's their perception that they did not get what they wanted or expected from your company, co-workers, etc. Knowing this, it makes it easier for you to focus on the solution rather than becoming defensive. If you've been making drinks the same way for years, and somebody's been drinking them for years, and then one day they say, "Hey, you know, this has too many strawberries in it." You may know in your heart of hearts that you've been making that drink exactly the same way and it's the exact same drink. That does not matter! What matters is that customer's perception in that moment. If they think, there are too many strawberries in the drink then that's the reality you deal with in that moment. You may say, "I apologize, was it too sweet? I'll get you another one right away." Your customer will perceive that you care about them and will be more compelled to continue doing business with you.

The biggest take away from this section is; don't make complaints personal, just make them right.

CHAPTER 8

Step 4: E Is For Empathy

E is for EMPATHY. What is empathy? Empathy is putting yourself into somebody else's shoes. Whether it's working with staff members or customers, this is how you connect to one another and build RAPPORT. When you can put yourself into someone else's shoes while you are communicating with them, that interaction shows the other person that you care. A couple of phrases that work are: "I know what you're going through, I've been there too." Or, "When I was in a similar situation, this is how I got through it." The easiest way to show EMPATHY is to remember a time when you were in a similar situation, think about how you felt and how you made it through the situation.

I was on the phone with the phone company a while back, and I was having a problem with my bill. The customer service representative said to me, "You know what? I've had problems with my bill too. I understand what you're going through, so I'm going to do everything I can to get this resolved for you." Just the fact that the customer service rep could relate to my problem made me feel connected and as though there is somebody on my side. That's showing empathy for your customers. Show concern for their challenge and let them know that you are going to do everything you can to get their problem taken care of accurately, fast and right.

Next, make sure you act APPROPRIATELY to the situation. We have talked a little bit about this before. If a customer is having an issue and you're just smiling in their face that may not go over so well. If they're concerned, show them that you're concerned too. Acknowledge that they have a valid concern and let them know that you will take care of this concern for them. Do you want to know the magical, secret phrase that is the beginning of ALL customer service conflict resolution?

Here it is: "I understand."

When somebody is really venting, and truly having an issue, show EMPATHY and say, "I understand." If it's true, you might add, "I've been there too" and that really helps convey that you know where they're coming from. A lot of times that all it takes to diffuse the situation. If not, at least you have a clear starting point at which to "wow" them with your resolution skills. More on that later.

CHAPTER 9

Step 5: C Is For Clarification

C is for CLARIFICATION. What is clarification and how does it relate to customer service? Once you UNDERSTAND the customer's needs or desires, clarify with the customer to make sure you got it right. If somebody orders a burger, fries and a drink, repeat it back to them. If someone orders your product in a particular size or color, read it back to him or her for CLARIFICATION that you have the order correct. Say, "Did I get that right?" "What I have for your order is..." It only takes an extra second or two, but CLARIFYING that you know exactly what the customer wants is priceless.

This will cut down on incorrect orders 80% or more depending on how you fulfill these orders. Sometimes, your customer will change their mind even after you have already CLARIFIED with them. That's okay. Simply make the change, thank the customer and continue on. On every order you take and in every interaction you have with the client, make sure you've done what you can to get that information CALRIFIED. This step will save you major headaches down the road.

Studies show that 95% of your unhappy customers will not tell you they're unhappy. They're not going to say anything. They won't complain to your manager, they won't make a big stink about it; they're just not going to come back. They're just going to disappear and there they go. All those marketing dollars you spent to acquire that person as a customer in the first place are lost. All because when they were here, you didn't take very good care of them. Make sure you are taking care of every customer by CLARIFYING their needs and checking in with them often to make sure they are happy throughout your process. You need to know what they want and they need to know that you are going to provide the exact solution for what they need in a friendly, efficient and accurate manner. Got it? Of course you do.

There are THREE KEY WAYS TO CLARIFY to clarify your customers' needs and wants. The first and easiest one is to REPEAT THEIR ORDER. Repeat what they're looking for from you and your company. If they're upset and complaining, get their story and repeat back what happened, as you UNDERSTAND it from your INTENT LISTENING. Now, this next part is crucial. CLARIFICATION is so important because you don't want to start working to solve a problem that your customer doesn't even have. It's so important I will repeat it again. YOU DON'T WANT TO START WORKING TO SOLVE A PROBLEM THAT YOUR CUSTOMER DOESN'T EVEN HAVE. Always make sure that you UNDERSTAND and CLARIFY exactly what the customer is telling you, what they want, what the problem is and what they expected. Compare the information that your client has given to you with the information you understand. Write it down if you have to and clarify it to make sure you got it.

The second key way to clarify is to confirm what the customer is ultimately trying to achieve. Ask yourself, "What are they ultimately trying to do or get?"

When you answer this question you will become resourceful in how to solve their issue through your SOLUTION, which we will talk about more in depth in the next section. Especially if you offer numerous products or services, you need to understand exactly what your client is trying to do. Do they need specific equipment that you offer, a specific service, advice, etc.? Once you are clear, then you can take them to the next step.

The third key is to repeat the SOLUTION back to the customer. If your customer has an issue, and you do come up with a remedy for them, you need to make sure that the remedy is going to make them happy. You may think to yourself, "I took care of that and the client should be happy." Your customer may be thinking, "They didn't take care of me at all. I am NOT happy." That client can now go and write a bad review, share their bad experience they had with the world; and by then it's too late. You may have been well intentioned and done your best to help the client, but all that truly matters is the client's perception. If they do not perceive that you took great care of them then you didn't. Period. Always make sure you clarify your SOLUTION with them and they agree to it.

TO BOOK YOUR NEXT LIVE TRAINING EVENT WITH DAVID BROWNLEE, CALL OR VISIT OUR WEBSITE TODAY!

(800) 299-3449

PureCustomerService.com

DavidBrownlee.com

CHAPTER 10

Step 6: S Is For Solution

FINALLY, S is for SOLUTION. Your goal as a customer service professional is to provide SOLUTIONS for your customers. That is your main function as a customer service professional, business owner or manager. You need to provide SOLUTIONS for your customers to get them their desired results. Whether the solution is an actual product or service or a remedy to an issue or a challenge.

There are THREE KEY WAYS to provide SOLUTIONS for your customers. THE FIRST KEY WAY is to DELIVER your product or service to your client. By DELIVER I don't mean shipping it to them necessarily, but transferring your SOLUTION from your company to your customer. You need to ensure that you DLEIVER the right product to your customer. Make sure your product or service does exactly what it claims to do and nothing less. Is it DELIVER it on time? Did your customer have to wait? If so, for how long? How will this affect their perception of the level of customer service they are receiving from you or your company? You had better have a good answer to these questions and really take the time to work out how to correct any deficiencies on this subject. When you are providing a service, ask yourself, "Is it the right service for your customer? Is it executed correctly? Is it the best quality service you can possibly provide?" Make sure your service does what it claims to do.

Deliver the REMEDY for your client's issue or problem. You need to make sure, though CLARIFYING that the remedy you come up with actually benefits your customer and that they agree with you. Really take a look at your REMEDY. Is it creative or special in anyway? Is your REMEDY going to create a "wow" moment for your customer? If they do have a problem and you fix it for them, did you just do the minimum to appease the customer, or did you go above and beyond what the customer expected?

Take a moment and think about a situation that has come up in your business and ask yourself this question. If you did the bare minimum to get them out of your hair, what could you have done differently to really "wow" your customer and turn them into a raving fan? What would you have done for Mick or Paul in this situation? Come up with a plan that will turn your customers into raving fans when they have a problem with your product or service. You'll love the results.

You could give a customer that had a problem that you fixed a coupon for the next time they come in. After you provide a REMEDY for your client, tell them, "We're really sorry that this went wrong for you, here's a coupon for the next time you come back and see us again." Give them something extra to make them say, "Okay, they screwed up, people are going to screw up, but they really took care of me and more than they took care of my problem."

Next, make sure the REMEDY you provide is the best remedy you can possibly provide. Remember, this should be engrained in your head by now; customers always leave the transaction happy! Even if they had an issue, you need to make absolutely sure that they are happy by the time they walk out of the door. You may even ask them "Is there anything else I can do to assist you?" Or, "Is there anything else you need?" "Would you like anything else?" This will also help you sell more products and services that may be an afterthought for your customers. For example, they may decide they want a desert to go or add an accessory to the cell phone they just bought, etc.

THE SECOND KEY WAY to deliver solutions is to FOLLOW UP with your customers. There are several ways to FOLLOW UP with your customers. You may choose one way or use a combination of ways. The first way is VERBALLY. Ask, "How was everything?" Your client may tell you, "You know, xyz wasn't quite right, or I would do xyz differently." Most customer service representatives do not ask this question because they are afraid of the answer. They are afraid and unsure of how to resolve a customer issue. At this point in the book, I know you are able to handle any situation!

When you get negative feedback, don't just say "Sorry" and move on. LISTEN, UNDERSTAND and CLARIFY specifically what the problem is and get to work on the REMEDY and the SOLUTION...immediately! Solve the issue yourself if you can or take it back to management right away.

Another way to FOLLOW UP with your customer is by using a comment card. These can be scary to customer service people. A lot of representatives, servers and managers are afraid of being told that they screwed up somehow, either the product or service. Now you have all of the tools you need to overcome any obstacle as far as customer issues and problems go. Practice these tools and remember to EMPATHIZE with your customers and then you'll know instinctively how to help them. We naturally have a tendency to only want to hear about the good stuff, we don't want to hear about the bad stuff. Take the negative comments as a time to really look at how you can improve your business in the future. Take every bad review and use it to change your process, procedures and standards in customer service.

When you get a comment card with a negative experience, reach out to that customer immediately. Catch them in the parking lot if you can, call them on the phone or send out an email. Your goal is to catch them and make things right with them before they get to Yelp or and online review sites. It is getting tougher and tougher to pull this off as more and more people are writing negative reviews from their smart phone while they are still sitting at your table! Tell them in person, via email or on the phone, "We're really sorry you didn't enjoy (whatever piece of our service that went wrong for you). We want to take care of you and make it right so we are offering you (some sort of discount, or come back in on us, or something). The point here being to TAKE ACTION ASAP! Do not wait until it's too late.

When following up with your customer, a live conversation in person or on the phone works best. Email is only the last resort. People are much more likely to respond favorably to a live conversation. Behind the email, they cannot hear the EMPATHY in your voice; see your facial expressions or any of the other nuances that show you really care about them as people. Depending on what industry you are in and your business interactions, you may have to adjust your FOLLOW UP procedures.

My favorite example of FOLLOWING UP on the phone is Enterprise Rent-a-Car. When you rent the car, because they hold such a high standard of customer service, they will call you on the phone just to see how your rental experience was. Before they close the rental branch for the night, they have the employees pick up the phone and call all of the customers who returned cars that day. Say what? Yup. There could be a lot of cars that come back at the end of their rental in one day. The associates make these calls until they finished (depending on the size and location of the branch). How would picking up the phone and checking in with your customers affect YOUR business? What if you called and said, "We just wanted to see how did everything go with you (product or service today)? Your customers would look at the phone like it was broken. "Say, what? Is this really happening?" Absolute delight ensues. This is how you step it up and "wow" your customers. Try it.

You can also FOLLOW UP with your customers via text message. There are some text messaging companies that can implement this system for you. It is not as personal as a conversation, but texts can get the feedback you're looking for quickly. "How did we do today?" "Would you recommend us to a friend?"

The easiest but least effective way to FOLLOW UP is email. However, email follow up is 1000% better than no follow up at all. Send your customers a thank you for visiting, and maybe send them a coupon for their next visit. Thanks for choosing us, please tell us how we did. You know, you can always put a survey in there as well. The challenge is getting someone to take the time to DO your survey. Make it one easy question. For example, "If you owned a customer service company, would you hire the person that helped you?" Bam.

The next way to FOLLOW UP is through an EMAIL DRIP CAMPAIGN. Every week, every month or every quarter, send an email to a list of your customers in which they get some sort of value. It could be discounts, coupons, advice, and information or just about anything your clients would appreciate receiving from you. This process keeps you top of mind for your clients, so they will think of you when they need your service. If you provide excellent value in the emails, they will absolutely feel CARED FOR. Postcards or direct mail are another way to FOLLOW UP with your customers and add value to them in some way.

THE THIRD KEY TO SOLUTIONS is to ANTICIPATE your customers' future needs. A great example of ANTICIPATING future needs of their customers is Netflix. When you order a movie on Netflix, something comes up on your screen that says "You liked "X" so you might also like "Y" and "Z." That is ANTICIPATING my needs.

The system anticipates what might benefit you by saving you time and suggesting something that has been selected just for you. If it looks good, you might click on it and add it to your queue. How convenient. Another great example of ANTICIPATING your clients' future needs is when you buy something from Amazon. Once you select your item, at the bottom of the screen it says, "People who bought what you are buying also bought this cool thing that relates to it in some way. That system also makes suggestions for you to make your life more convenient. This especially relevant in a society where everything is now, now, now!

Take a close look at what your clients are buying and make suggestions to them that will help make their life more convenient, enhance the performance of the widget you just sold to them, etc. Not only will you increase your revenues, you'll also serve your client at an even higher level.

For more information on our SALES TRAINING PROGRAMS, visit DavidBrownlee.com

I covered a lot of this in sections, so here are the highlights:

a. Look at the purchase history for customers and make suggestions based on that data.
b. Suggest companion items.
c. Update your service based on feedback received from conversations, comment cards, emails, surveys or texts.

TO BOOK YOUR NEXT LIVE TRAINING EVENT WITH DAVID BROWNLEE, CALL OR VISIT OUR WEBSITE TODAY!

(800) 299-3449

PureCustomerService.com

DavidBrownlee.com

CHAPTER 11

What's next?

WOW! That was fun. I know you learned a lot from this book and are ready to implement it in your business or career, right? Of course you are. Take a moment, and ask yourself, "What's possible for me and business when I implement these 6 steps?" Visualize the certainty you and your staff will have in knowing exactly how to handle any customer service challenge that comes up. You are rock stars! Now you know how to gain customer referrals, improve your online reviews, grow your customer base and increase your revenues!

WOULD YOU LIKE THE WORKBOOK AND QUIZ THAT ACCOMPANY THIS E- BOOK?

Call us today to find out how to get your copy (800) 299-3449.

Did you already purchase **The Rock Star Customer Service Training Program**? If not, the program takes all of the great concepts in this book and puts them all together for you in a fun, informative and kick ass-training course! If you have not already ordered the training, you can find it here:

RockStarCustomerService.com

Are you ready to take your organization to the next level?

Hire David Brownlee to come speak to your organization or train your staff live. Call for more information (800) 299-3449.

Thanks for reading, now get out there and serve your clients!

A PERSONAL NOTE FROM AVID BROWNLEE

—

Hi there,

Have you ever had these challenges before? Do you ever wonder why you are not getting the customer referrals you would like to get in your business and not retaining the customers you already have? You know you need to increase your revenues but you've tried everything and have no clue how to do it?

ME too. No one ever taught me how to do these things when I started my first company. If you don't know my story, I got my bachelor's degree in speech communications from California State University Northridge. Then, after college I joined the corporate world like I thought I was supposed to do at the time. I learned a lot, had some great training, but I wasn't really happy inside. I didn't feel fulfilled. I enjoyed helping my customers but going into the office every day, sitting in my cubicle and going through the motions sent me into a depression. I knew I wanted to start my own entertainment and special event planning business and be my own boss, but I didn't know where to start. As I became more down on myself, the worse things got my relationship at the time ended badly, and I ended up living in my best friend's dining room on the floor of his apartment. I had a little mattress that I put there and would sleep on every night. That was it. I had literally hit rock bottom. Some point that after listening to me complaining day in and day out, he convinced me to go for it, and start my company (I'm sure was excited to have his dining room back too), but I went for it.

Small businesses and entrepreneurs today are frustrated with customer service ideas that just don't work. They have spent thousands of dollars on online marketing, print, business directories and none of those things are making them any money and not getting them more customers. My client's come to me that they are fed up with waiting for their Facebook and Twitter accounts to start spewing money. I've got news for you, it most likely not going to happen. Although, I think social media is very important for businesses, it rarely brings in substantial money on its own; with a few exceptions of course.

I created this book to explain what I've found through personal experience and years of studying this subject and talking with successful business owners, CEO's and entrepreneurs.

I ended up building a business where I went from absolutely NOTHING to making over SIX FIGURES in 12 months. I went from living on the dining room floor of my buddy's apartment to owning my own home and travelling the world. I figured out what it takes to grow a business and create freedom for yourself, so you can enjoy life. It took me countless hours of studying and researching to crack that code and I made a lot of mistakes along the way. I wish THIS program would have existed when I was building that first company. It would have saved me thousands of dollars and valuable time.

I've used that same code and foundation to build and sell other businesses since then. Now you have the opportunity to take an advantage of what I've learned and picked up along the way from the most successful people in business. Hands down, Rock Star Marketing Mastery and understanding your clients' needs is the secret sauce. That's the foundation for building an outstanding business or taking your career to the next level. Once you understand the secrets of how to do this, your life will change forever.

The US Army, CVS, T-Mobile, universities and more have used my trainings!

I tell you this story not to impress you, but to impress upon you that if I can do it, you can do it too. There are a few simple fundamentals that you must master and then you'll have the opportunity to have more freedom, travel, spend time with your family and friends or anything else you desire.

Thank you for reading and I hope you got the great value from this book! To continue your education and close the gap from where you are now to where you want to be, call or email us today!

Sincerely,

David Brownlee

(800) 299-3449

PureCustomerService.com

DavidBrownlee.com

Earnings Disclaimer:

We don't believe in "get rich" programs – only in hard work, adding value, building a real and professional career, and serving others with excellence and constancy. Our programs are intended to help you provide your customers with excellent customer service and to make a difference in your market while growing your brand. Our programs take a lot of work and discipline just like any worthwhile endeavor or professional continuing education program. Please don't purchase our programs if you believe in the "money for nothing get rich quick" myth or ideology; we only want serious people dedicated to real professional development who want to add value and move humanity forward. As stipulated by law, we cannot and do not make any guarantees about your ability to get results or earn any money with our ideas, information, tools or strategies. We don't know you and, besides, your results in life are up to you. Agreed?

We just want to help by giving great content, direction, and strategies. What we can guarantee is your satisfaction; we give you a 30-day 100% satisfaction guarantee, so if you are not happy for any reason with the quality of our training, just ask for your money back. You should know that all products and services by our company are for educational and informational purposes only. Nothing on this page, any of our websites, books, MP3's, PDF's or any of our content or curriculum is a promise or guarantee of results or future earnings, and we do not offer any legal, medical, tax or other professional advice. Any financial numbers referenced here, or on any of our sites, are illustrative of concepts only and should not be considered average earnings, exact earnings, or promises for actual or future performance.

Making decisions based on any information presented in our products, events, services, or web site, should be done only with the knowledge that you could experience risk or losses just like any entrepreneurial endeavor. Use caution and always consult your accountant, lawyer or professional advisor before acting on this or any information related to a lifestyle change or your business or finances. You alone are responsible and accountable for your decisions, actions and results in life, and by your registration here you agree not to attempt to hold us liable for your decisions, actions or results, at any time, under any circumstance.

www.ingramcontent.com/pod-product-compliance
Lightning Source LLC
Chambersburg PA
CBHW021923170526
45157CB00005B/2157